Story of My Life

RESTORING A POSITIVE SENSE OF SELF
THROUGH
SELF DISCOVERY JOURNALING

By: Channing Clark, M.A., LCPC

Restore You Media
8101 Sandy Spring Rd.
Laurel, MD 20707
www.restoreyoucounseling.com
contactus@restoreyoucounseling.com
ISBN: 978-0-578-74571-8
Copyright © 2020 by Restore You Media

Disclaimer

This book is designed to provide information and motivation to our readers. It is sold with the understanding that the author and publisher are not engaged to render any type of psychological, legal, or any other kind of professional advice. Therefore, it is not intended to diagnose, treat, cure, or prevent any condition or disease. You understand that this book is not intended as a substitute for consultation with a licensed practitioner. Please consult with your physician or healthcare specialist regarding the suggestions and recommendations made in this book. The publisher and the author are providing this book and its contents on an "as is" basis and make no representations or warranties of any kind with respect to this book or its contents. The publisher and author make no guarantees concerning the level of success you may experience by following the advice and strategies contained in this book, and you accept the risk that results will differ for each individual. The use of this book implies your acceptance of this disclaimer. This publication is meant as a source of valuable information and resources for the reader, however, it is not meant as a substitute for direct expert assistance. If such a level of assistance is required, the services of a competent professional should be sought.

Table of Contents

Preface

Have you ever talked with someone and as they share their story it leaves you in shock? You're at a loss for words with chills crawling up your spine because as they give the detail of their experiences it is as if they were reading a page from your diary. Well, I have, and this experience was the inspiration for this journal. "Story of my life" is an expression my best friend and I have been tossing back and forth for years. It's a simple phrase that we use to indicate that a specific pattern of behaviors resembles our own. Typically, we don't recognize the pattern until we hear others tell their story. However, as a mental health professional, I'm fully aware of how our patterns, both good and bad, have a major impact on one's quality of life. With the "Story of My Life Journal," you are equipped with a tool to help readers to identify unhealthy patterns in order to address and resolve them. The goal of the "Story of My Life Journal" is to guide the reader through their internal processes such as their thoughts, feelings, and behaviors with the hopes of identifying and resolving unhealthy patterns in one's life in order to enhance their quality of life. While this journal can be used for personal use, however, it is recommended that readers use these journals along with a mental health professional to enhance the process.

Creating this book began with many clients that I have encouraged to journal, but they often found themselves stuck on where to start or just plain outright said "It's not my thing." However, for those who gave it a try, I've seen those completely opposed to journaling embrace the tool with open arms. Writing is truly therapeutic and the benefits of journaling can last a lifetime. I believe journaling opens the portal of our minds to the unconscious thoughts, desires, and regrets that our behaviors attempt to reveal to us. It is my belief that all behavior comes from somewhere. Yet, too often we are so busy with our lives that we don't pay attention to our behaviors or lack thereof that speak on behalf of our unconscious self. When we are able to bring forth our hidden selves we can unravel the negative patterns and cycles that consume our lives.

This 31-day journaling guide provides you with daily journaling prompts for those who are new to journaling or want to add to their journaling repertoire.

NOw LEt the Journaling Begin!

How to Use This Book

Welcome, to the beginning of your self-discovery journal! Below you will find an explanation for the items in this journal.:

Quote

Each day starts with a quote that is meant to start the process of provoking thoughts and content for that day's journaling entry.

Tip: Don't rush past the quote. Feel free to read and reread the quote to write what the quote is speaking to you.

Feelings

Here I provide you with a list of 5 emotions to select from for the day. While in one day you could probably circle all 5 emotions. It is recommended to circle the emotion that stood out to you the most in the day. Or which emotion lasted the longest in that day.

Tip: It's important not to skip this step because you will use this information later.

Writing Prompt

This is pretty self-explanatory, but I'll continue anyway. In this section, I've developed questions for you to think and write about.

Tip: Please don't feel confined to these writing prompts this is to get your mind thinking, but as you write other thoughts may come up and feel free to go with those thoughts in your writing.

Lesson

At the end of each day's journal entry, I've left space to write about what lesson you learned about yourself, others, or the world. This provides the opportunity to explore the different experiences you had in the day and describe what you would appreciate, learned, and/or what you would like to change about yourself, others, or the world.

How to Use This Book

Weekly Reflection
This section is used to gather information regarding your feelings from the last seven journal entries. Space is provided before each feeling for you to put a number that indicates how many days you experienced each corresponding feeling.

Tip: As you go back to track your feelings feel free to review some of your journal entries as well to explore where those feelings come from.

Weekly Life Satisfaction Survey
This survey allows you to take a moment to reflect on eight areas (i.e. self, health, relationships, finances, career, emotions, fun, and spirituality) of your life. Using a Likert scale you provide a self-report of how satisfied you are with your current state in those areas.

Tip: There is no right or wrong answer to this survey. This is simply to track areas that you aren't satisfied with and explore ways to improve in those areas.

Overall Life Satisfaction Survey
This survey is a place in which you can review all of your previous life Satisfaction Surveys to identify areas of growth and continued challenging areas.

Tip: This survey allows you to hold yourself accountable for the goals that you have set in order to improve your overall life satisfaction.

Day 1

There is no right way to write. In writing, you start with a letter and the words will follow.

Date: _____

Select the feeling that best describes how you felt today?

Love   Joy   Anger   Sadness   Fear

Writing Prompts:

Be free today. Write whatever you're thinking. Don't think about spelling, grammar, or whether or not it makes sense. Simply write.

What challenges did you experience today?

What positive things happened today?

What lesson about yourself, others, and/or the world did you learn from today?

Day 2

The answers that you need are within.

Date: _____

Select the feeling that best describes how you felt today?

Love   Joy   Anger   Sadness   Fear

Writing Prompts:

Today let's take a look inside. Close your eyes and think about your day from the beginning to end. Write the moments of your day that meant the most to you.

Identify and describe the event(s) that caused the feeling that you selected today.

_____

_____

_____

_____

_____

_____

_____

_____

_____

_____

_____

_____

_____

_____

_____

_____

_____

_____

_____

_____

_____

Describe an event from the past that has caused a similar feeling to the one you selected today.

What lesson did you learn about yourself, others, and/or the world today?

Day 3

Love yourself. You're worth it.

Date: _____

Select the feeling that best describes how you felt today?

Love   Joy   Anger   Sadness   Fear

Writing Prompts:

Take a moment or two and look into the mirror as you reflect on the following writing prompts.:

What do you love about yourself?

_____

_____

_____

_____

_____

_____

_____

_____

_____

_____

_____

_____

_____

What would the world be missing if you weren't here?

What makes you unique?

What lesson did you learn about yourself, others, and/or the world today?

Day 4

Digging is hard work, however, once you find what you're looking for the work is but a distant memory.

Date: _____

Select the feeling that best describes how you felt today?

Love   Joy   Anger   Sadness   Fear

Writing Prompts:

It's time to do some digging. Our past provides us with a wealth of information. If we don't understand our past thoughts and behaviors then we are likely to repeat them.

Describe your earliest memory.

How did you feel at the time of the early memory you described
in the previous writing prompt?

Describe any experiences from your past that are similar to the memory you have described.

What lesson did you learn about yourself, others, and/or the
world today?

Day 5

You can find peace, if you are willing to find it.

Date: _____

Select the feeling that best describes how you felt today?

Love   Joy   Anger   Sadness   Fear

Writing Prompts:

Peace looks and feels different for everyone. Use these writing prompts to identify what peace looks like for you.

Describe a time and/or place when you felt at peace

_____

_____

_____

_____

_____

_____

_____

_____

_____

_____

_____

_____

_____

_____

_____

_____

_____

_____

What made that time and/or place peaceful?

Use your imagination and create your own perfect peaceful
environment. What does it look, smell, or feel like?

What lesson did you learn about yourself, others, and the world today?

Day 6

The only thing that should happen over night is sleeping.
Everyting else takes patient endurance.

Date: _____

Select the feeling that best describes how you felt today?

Love   Joy   Anger   Sadness   Fear

Writing Prompts:

What are your personal and professional goals?

What are the steps needed to reach those goals?

What steps can you begin to work on tomorrow?
How can you overcome the barriers to take theses steps?

Day 7

A song a week

Date: _ _ _ _ _ _ _ _ _ _ _ _ _

Select the feeling that best describes how you felt today?

Love   Joy   Anger   Sadness   Fear

Writing Prompts:
Sit back and listen to a song with your eyes closed.
What does the song say, mean, and/or feel to you?

What lesson did you learn about yourself, others, and
the world today?

Day 8

Time of Reflection

Date: _____

Review your past 7 days of journal entries and answer the following questions.

How many days did you feel:

Love? _____   Joy? _____   Anger? _____
Sadness? _____   Fear ? _____

Can you identify any concerns or improvements with your feelings in the past 7 days?

_____

_____

_____

_____

_____

_____

_____

_____

_____

_____

_____

_____

_____

What patterns can you identify in your journal entries?

What lessons have you learned in the past 7 days?

Life Satisfaction Survey

Use the scale below to identify how satisfied you feel in the following areas of life.

	1 Very Dissatisfied	2 Dissatisfied	3 Satisfied	4 Very Satisfied
Self	1.	2.	3.	4
Health	1.	2.	3.	4
Relationships	1.	2.	3.	4
Finances	1.	2.	3.	4
Career	1.	2.	3.	4
Emotions	1.	2.	3.	4
Fun	1.	2.	3.	4
Spirituality	1.	2.	3.	4

Identify one area of life that you would like to work on improving in the next 7 days. Describe what you will do differently in the next 7 days.

_____

_____

_____

_____

_____

_____

_____

_____

_____

_____

Keep
JOURNALING!!

It keeps your mood

&

It keeps your stress

Day 9

"The value of life lies not in the length of days, but in. the use we make of them."

Michel De Montaigne

Date: _____

Select the feeling that best describes how you felt today?

Love   Joy   Anger   Sadness   Fear

Writing Prompts:
What matters most to you in life?

_____
_____
_____
_____
_____
_____
_____
_____
_____
_____
_____
_____
_____
_____

What lesson did you learn about yourself, others, and/or the world today?

Day 10

"You only live once, but if you do it right, once is enough."
Mae West

Date: _____

Select the feeling that best describes how you felt today?

Love   Joy   Anger   Sadness   Fear

Writing Prompts:

Are you living a life true to yourself? If so, how? If not, why?

What lesson did you learn about yourself, others, and/or the world today?

Day 11

"Love cures people -
both the ones who give it and the ones who receive it."
Karl Menninger

Date: _____

Select the feeling that best describes how you felt today?

Love   Joy   Anger   Sadness   Fear

Writing Prompts:

Make a list of people in life who support you and whom you trust. If you do
not have anyone your trust write about what it would take to have a
trusting relationship.

What lesson did you learn about yourself, others, and/or the world today?

Day 12

"Change will not come if we wait for some other person or some other time. We are the ones we've been waiting for. We are the change that we seek."
Barack Obama

Date: _____

Select the feeling that best describes how you felt today?

Love   Joy   Anger   Sadness   Fear

Writing Prompts:
Make a list of everything you'd like to say no to.
Make a list of everything you'd like to say yes to.

Now write about what is keeping you from saying yes and /or no.

What lessons did you learn about yourself, others,
and/or the world today?

Day 13

Nobody can love you like you can.

Date: _____

Select the feeling that best describes how you felt today?

Love   Joy   Anger   Sadness   Fear

Writing Prompts:

Many times we can lean towards others for emotional support . Take a
moment to provide yourself with support.
What do you need to hear today?

What lesson did you learn about yourself others, and/or the world today?

Day 14

Let's Make a Wish...

Date: _____

Select the feeling that best describes how you felt today?

Love   Joy   Anger   Sadness   Fear

Writing Prompts:
Finish the following sentences:
I wish I felt...
I wish I had....
I wish I could....

What lesson did you learn about yourself, others, and/or the world today?

Day 15

A song a week

Date: _____

Select the feeling that best describes how you felt today?

Love   Joy   Anger   Sadness   Fear

Writing Prompts:
Sit back and listen to a song with your eyes closed.
What does the song say, mean, and/or feel to you?

What lesson did you learn about yourself, othes, and/or. the world today?

Day 16

Time of Reflection

Date: _____

Review your past 7 days of journal entries and answer the following questions.

How many days did you feel:

Love? _____   Joy? _____   Anger? _____
Sadness? _____   Fear ? _____

Below add together the "Time of Reflection" from Day 8 and the one above and place the total number of days for each feeling since starting the journal.

Love? _____   Joy? _____   Anger? _____
Sadness? _____   Fear ? _____

Can you identify any concerns or improvements with your feelings since the last "Time of Reflection?"

What patterns can you identify in your journal entries?

What lessons have you learned in the past 7 days?

LIfe Satisfaction Survey

Use the scale below to identify how satisfied you feel in the following areas of life.

1 Very Dissatisfied	2 Dissatisfied	3 Satisfied	4 Very Satisfied
Self	1.	2.	3.	4
Health	1.	2.	3.	4
Relationships	1.	2.	3.	4
Finances	1.	2.	3.	4
Career	1.	2.	3.	4
Emotions	1.	2.	3.	4
Fun	1.	2.	3.	4
Spirituality	1.	2.	3.	4

Identify one area of life that you would like to work on improving in the next 7 days. Describe what you will do differently in the next 7 days.

LIfe Satisfaction Survey
Follow Up
Review your last LIfe Satisfaction Survey and answer the following questions:

Has there been any progress and/or challenges with improving your life satisfaction since the last survey?

Keep
JOURNALING!!

It helps with your memory

Day 17

No man can measure the weight one's mind carries.

Date: _ _ _ _ _ _ _ _ _ _ _ _ _

Select the feeling that best describes how you felt today?

Love   Joy   Anger   Sadness   Fear

Writing Prompt:

Today let's do a mind dump. Start writing and allow your thoughts to flow naturally. Even if you have to start by writing "I don't know what to write."

What lesson did you learn about yourself, others, and/or the world today?

Day 18

"The bliss of existence is a blessed excursion through time."
— Lailah Gifty Akita

Date: _____

Select the feeling that best describes how you felt today?

Love   Joy   Anger   Sadness   Fear

Writing Prompts:
Imagine your life story was a book. What would be the title? And why?

What lesson did you learn about yourself, others, and/or the world today?

Day 19

Give Thanks!

Date: _____

Select the feeling that best describes how you felt today?

Love   Joy   Anger   Sadness   Fear

Writing Prompts:

It can be easy to recall the negative events in our lives. Take today to reflect
on the positive memories and moments in your life. Make a list of at least 10
things that you are thankful for.

What lesson did you learn about yourself, others, and/or the world today?

Day 20

Let's Dream!

Date: _ _ _ _ _ _ _ _ _ _ _ _ _

Select the feeling that best describes how you felt today?

Love   Joy   Anger   Sadness   Fear

Writing Prompts:

Take a moment and imagine that you have an endless amount of money and no need to work. If this were the case, how would you spend your time?

Whalt lesson did you learn about yourself, others, and/or the world today?

Day 21

Let's Make a Wish!

Date: _____

Select the feeling that best describes how you felt today?

Love   Joy   Anger   Sadness   Fear

Writing Prompts:
Finish the following statements.

Life should be about....

I am going to make life about....

I am courageous when....

What lesson did you learn about yourself, others, and/or the world today?

Day 22

One of the best places to find wisdom is in one's past.

***

Date: _ _ _ _ _ _ _ _ _ _ _ _ _

Select the feeling that best describes how you felt today?

Love   Joy   Anger   Sadness   Fear

Writing Prompts:

Let's imagine you were given one opportunity to go back to your past and tell yourself something. What period of your life would you go to? What would you say to yourself?

_____

_____

_____

_____

_____

_____

_____

_____

_____

_____

_____

_____

_____

_____

_____

_____

What lesson did you learn about yourself, others, and/or the world today?

Day 23
A song a week

Date: _____

Select the feeling that best describes how you felt today?

Love   Joy   Anger   Sadness   Fear

Writing Prompts:
Sit back and listen to a song with your eyes closed.
What does the song say, mean, and/or feel to you?

What lesson did you learn about yourself, others, and/or the world today?

Day 24
Time of Reflection

Date: _____

Review your past 7 days of journal entries and answer the following questions.

How many days did you feel:

Love? _____   Joy? _____   Anger? _____
Sadness? _____   Fear ? _____

Below add together the "Time of Reflection" from Day 8 and the one above and place the total number of days for each feeling since starting the journal.

Love? _____   Joy? _____   Anger? _____
Sadness? _____   Fear ? _____

Can you identify any concerns or improvements with your feelings since the last "Time of Reflection?"

What patterns can you identify in your journal entries?

What lessons have you learned in the past 7 days?

Life Satisfaction Survey

Use the scale below to identify how satisfied you feel in the following areas of life.

	1 Very Dissatisfied	2 Dissatisfied	3 Satisfied	4 Very Satisfied
Self	1.	2.	3.	4
Health	1.	2.	3.	4
Relationships	1.	2.	3.	4
Finances	1.	2.	3.	4
Career	1.	2.	3.	4
Emotions	1.	2.	3.	4
Fun	1.	2.	3.	4
Spirituality	1.	2.	3.	4

Identify one area of life that you would like to work on improving in the next 7 days. Describe what you will do differently in the next 7 days.

_____

_____

_____

_____

_____

_____

_____

_____

_____

LIfe Satisfaction Survey
Follow Up
Review your last LIfe Satisfaction Survey and answer the following questions:

Has there been any progress and/or challenges with improving your life satisfaction since the last survey?

KEEP
JOURNALING!!

It can bring

&

clear your
MIND

Day 25

"It's amazing how a little tomorrow can make up for a whole lot of yesterday."
— John Guare, Landscape of the Body

Date: _____

Select the feeling that best describes how you felt today?

Love   Joy   Anger   Sadness   Fear

Writing Prompts:

Today let's have a talk with our future. Based on the lessons learned from the past, write a letter to your future self.

What lessons have you learned about yourself, others, and./or the world today?

Day 26

Success is to be measured not so much by the position that one has reached in life as by the obstacles which he has overcome."
Booker T. Washington

Date: _____

Select the feeling that best describes how you felt today?

Love   Joy   Anger   Sadness   Fear

Writing Prompts:

What are some of the challenges that you have faced and overcome in your life?

What lesson did you learn about yourself, others, and/or the world today?

Day 27

"We have to be honest about what we want and take risks rather than lie to ourselves and make excuses to stay in our comfort zone."
— Roy T. Bennett, The Light in the Heart

Date: _____

Select the feeling that best describes how you felt today?

Love   Joy   Anger   Sadness   Fear

Writing Prompts:
Identify and discuss at least three things you can do to step outside of your comfort zone.

What lesson did you learn today about yourself, others, and/or the world today?

Day 28

"Start each day with a positive thought and a grateful heart."
— Roy T. Bennett,

Date: _ _ _ _ _ _ _ _ _ _ _ _ _

Select the feeling that best describes how you felt today?

Love   Joy   Anger   Sadness   Fear

Writing Prompts:

It's time to do some research. Identify at least two positive affirmations that speak to you and jot them down below.

What lesson did you learn about yourself, others, and the world today?

Day 29

Three things in human life are important:
The first is to be kind.
The second is to be kind.
And the third is to be kind.
Henry James

Date: _ _ _ _ _ _ _ _ _ _ _ _ _

Select the feeling that best describes how you felt today?

Love   Joy   Anger   Sadness   Fear

Writing Prompts:

Acts of kindness not only help the one that receives them it also helps the one who gives it. Make a list of some acts of kindness that you can do this week.

What lesson did you learn about yourself, others, and/or the world today?

Day 30

A song a week

Date: _____

Select the feeling that best describes how you felt today?

Love   Joy   Anger   Sadness   Fear

Writing Prompts:
Sit back and listen to a song with your eyes closed.
What does the song say, mean, and/or feel to you?

What lesson did you learn about yourself, others, and/or the world today?

Day 31

Time of Reflection

Date: _____

Review your past 7 days of journal entries and answer the following questions.

How many days did you feel:

Love? _____   Joy? _____   Anger? _____
Sadness? _____   Fear ? _____

Below add together the "Time of Reflection" from Day 8 and the one above and place the total number of days for each feeling since starting the journal.

Love? _____   Joy? _____   Anger? _____
Sadness? _____   Fear ? _____

Can you identify any concerns or improvements with your feelings since the last "Time of Reflection?"

What patterns can you identify in your journal entries?

What lessons have you learned in the past 7 days?

Life Satisfaction Survey

Use the scale below to identify how satisfied you feel in the following areas of life.

	1 Very Dissatisfied	2 Dissatisfied	3 Satisfied	4 Very Satisfied
Self	1.	2.	3.	4
Health	1.	2.	3.	4
Relationships	1.	2.	3.	4
Finances	1.	2.	3.	4
Career	1.	2.	3.	4
Emotions	1.	2.	3.	4
Fun	1.	2.	3.	4
Spirituality	1.	2.	3.	4

Identify one area of life that you would like to work on improving in the next 7 days. Describe what you will do differently in the next 7 days.

LIfe Satisfaction Survey
Follow Up
Review your last LIfe Satisfaction Survey and answer the following questions:

Has there been any progress and/or challenges with improving your life satisfaction since the last survey?

Keep
JOURNALING!!

It can help

LET **GO**

of the negative

EMBRACE the

POSITIVE

THE END...
OR IS IT?

Pat yourself on the back because you have officially started your journaling journey, but don't stop here. You can keep the momentum going just grab a pen and paper and start writing.

As mentioned at the beginning of this book it is recommended that you work along with a mental health professional to enhance the process. Some of the journaling prompts may have brought to the surface some thoughts and feelings you may want to consult with a mental health professional to explore those thoughts and feelings in depth.

Let the JOURNALING continue!

Tell me what your journaling journey was like by tagging us on Instagram and Facebook @Restoreyoucc.
You can find additional resources and information at www.restoreyoucounseling.com.